Closing the Gap
Bridging Differences through the Art of Negotiation

Blaise Glenn Bell

Table of Contents

Negotiation in the classic diplomatic sense assumes parties more anxious to agree than to disagree.

— Dean Acheson

Chapter 1. Introduction

Immerse yourself in the dynamic world of negotiation as we uncover the power it possesses in bridging diverse opinions, ethnicities, genders, and more in our Special Report: "Closing the Gap: Bridging Differences through the Art of Negotiation." This is no dry, technical exposition of facts, but a vibrant journey through real-life stories, tangible tools and strategies. This report illustrates how the art of negotiation can transform potentially divisive situations into catalysts for unity, understanding, and mutual progress. Whether you're a corporate leader, a public speaker, or simply someone trying to navigate through daily conflicts, this report is your beacon. Offering a fresh, insightful perspective on negotiation, this report promises to both educate and inspire. By the time you reach the end, you won't just want to buy this report, you'll want to share its treasures with everyone you know. Dive in, and let us help you change the world, one negotiation at a time.

Chapter 2. The Essence of Negotiation: A Comprehensive Introduction

Negotiation is a term that is often tossed around in various fields, from business to politics, and from conflict resolution to consumer dealings. Its universal application is a testament to its significance in the broader societal framework.

2.1. Understanding Negotiation

Negotiation, by definition, is the process of engaging in dialogues or discussions with the intention of reaching an agreement or compromise. This definition, while accurate, is the mere tip of the iceberg. Any attempt to box and wrap the concept of negotiation into a simple, definitive sentence would be a disservice to its profound depth and considerable breadth.

The essence of negotiation is constantly evolving, adapting, and morphing into multiple dimensions as a direct reflection of the multifaceted human society. To truly fathom, it is vital to embark on an exploratory journey that delves into its underlying layers.

2.2. The Multifaceted Nature of Negotiation

Negotiation is a dynamic process that involves multiple stages, each commanding a distinct set of skills from the negotiators. From preparation, where parties ascertain and outline their needs and wants, to the exchange of proposals, where bids are shared, examined, and revised, to the bargaining, where concessions and compromises are made, the complexity of negotiation unfolds sequentially. Such multistage composition of negotiation illustrates its intrinsic malleability and ascertains its role as a skill, as much as a science.

Apart from its procedural complexity, negotiation exhibits a significant behavioural dimension, our human instinct, to cooperate or compete, to listen or to speak, factors in significantly during a negotiation process. It's a dance between the logical and the emotional, the rational and the intuitive, the explicit and the implicit.

2.3. The Role of Power in Negotiation

One salient aspect of the negotiation process is the distribution of power. Oftentimes, when thinking about power in negotiation, one might be lured into equating it with authority or control. However, in the realm of negotiation, influence trumps control, suggesting that the power to persuade, to inspire, to connect, and to empathize often determines the success of the negotiation.

Power procurement in negotiation is a byproduct of different elements, the chief of which are knowledge, patience, optionality and empathy. Here, the practical manifestation of the old dictum, "knowledge is power," is eloquently evident.

2.4. Negotiation and Conflict Resolution

Negotiation is also a vital tool for conflict resolution. Be it political disputes between nations or everyday disagreements, negotiation serves as the bridge that spans the chasm between divergent stances. While disagreements are a natural occurrence within any dynamic interaction, it is the management of such conflicts what determines the health and the success of relationships. This is where negotiation sweeps in, transforming potential contention points into convergent objectives and shared interests.

While negotiation is integral to conflict resolution, it is important to understand that negotiation is not synonymous with dispute settlement. It goes much beyond that. It is about exploring creative solutions, fostering understanding, and nurturing relationships.

2.5. Intrinsic Human Connection in Negotiation

Negotiation can seem a ruthless game of winner-takes-all if held under the traditional, transactional microscope. However, the exploration of its essence points towards an indispensable human connection. Empathy, integrity, respect, and authenticity are key ingredients that furnish negotiation with a humane spirit, empowering it to rise above individual gains and encompass collective growth.

2.6. Key Take Away

Understanding the essence of negotiation is crucial in forming our attitudes and strategies as we navigate our way through life's myriad interactions. As we have seen, negotiation is not merely reaching a compromise or closing a deal. It is a multidimensional process that involves tactful negotiation, cognitive flexibility, understanding of human behaviour, smart management of power dynamics, conflict resolution, and fostering of intrinsic human connection.

This holistic understanding of negotiation helps establish it not just as an important life skill, but also as a powerful tool that could potentially shape interpersonal relationships, corporate dynamics, national policies, and even international diplomacy.

And with that, we have laid the groundwork upon which we will construct the subsequent chapters, each of which will delve deeper into specific aspects of negotiation and equip you with an enriched understanding and concrete strategies to become a master negotiator.

Chapter 3. The Anatomy of Differences: Identifying and Understanding the Gaps

The world thrives on differences. It is this variety that adds richness, diversity, and dynamism to our everyday existence. However, while these differences bring a beautiful heterogeneity to humanity, they can also give rise to conflicts, disagreements, and misunderstandings. Diversity is a double-edged sword, a harmonious symphony of distinct voices when understood, a discordant cacophony when not. It is thus that we commence our journey, tackling head-on, the anatomy of differences, tracing their origins, identifying them, and understanding their underlying nuances.

3.1. The Nature of Differences: A Fundamental Understanding

There are numerous differences that exist between individuals, dictated by variables such as culture, ethnicity, gender, socio-economic background, education, personal beliefs, and experiences. These individual characteristics shape our perspective and world view, defining our ways of communication, conflict resolution, decision-making processes, and consequently, our approach to negotiation.

To truly grasp the essence of these differences, one needs to traverse beyond the surface, down to the roots where they stem from. There is a certain school of thought that propounds that differences are largely derived from socio-cultural conditioning. This includes factors such as the environment we were raised in, the values inculcated by our parents, the influence of peers, the education we've had, life's experiences, and our subjective interpretations of the world.

Then there are inherent differences, attributed to our genetic make-up. Often these intrinsic disparities are hard to identify due to their subtle nature, yet they significantly impact our behavioral traits, emotional responses, and cognitive abilities.

While it might be tempting to categorize the differences into neatly compartmentalized boxes, it's more realistic to view them as a complex, interwoven fabric, a mosaic where each individual piece contributes to the overall pattern.

3.2. Identifying Differences: The Art and Science

If you are to bridge the divide successfully, you must first be able to recognize the breadth and depth of the differences you're dealing with. It makes the critical difference between addressing the root cause and simply applying a cosmetic fix.

Identifying differences can be an art as well as a science, built on a base of acute observation, empathetic understanding, patience, open-mindedness, and cultural competency. It involves listening, not just to spoken words, but to the resonating moods, emotions, and undercurrents. Watching, not just the explicit actions, but the subtle body language, the tiny nuances in expressions, the non-verbal cues. Think, not just in terms of self-centric views, but from the perspective of the 'other,' with empathy, and genuine willingness to understand.

As much as this is an art, it borders on being a science as well. It calls for the systematic understanding of human psychology, familiarity with context-specific parameters, and knowledge of socio-cultural factors at play. Tools like the Meyers-Briggs Type Indicator (MBTI) or the Thomas-Kilmann Conflict Mode Instrument (TKI) can be employed for empirical assessments of differences.

A word of caution here. Identifying differences does not mean enforcing stereotypes. Each individual is unique, and while one may identify common patterns within groups, it is crucial not to overlook individual variances.

3.3. Understanding the Gaps: The Key to Bridging them

Once you've identified the differences, the next step is to bridge them. But before a bridge can be built, it's imperative to comprehend the breadth, depth, complexity, and impact of the gap that these differences have created.

Understanding gaps involves considering the ways in which these differences affect communication, create barriers, breed misunderstandings, and potentially escalate into conflicts. It implies recognizing the power dynamics, socio-political contexts, implicit biases, and pre-conditioned stereotypes that come into play.

This is not just about understanding 'what' the gaps are, but also 'why' they exist. What underlying fears, insecurities, or prejudices are at work? What historical, cultural or personal contexts are influencing these gaps?

Understanding these gaps does not come without its challenges. It involves shaking off the shackles of your biases, shedding the comfort of your preconceived notions, and unlearning years of conditioned responses. However, it's worth every bit of effort because it allows you to view the negotiation from an informed perspective.

In conclusion, comprehending the anatomy of differences involves identifying these differences and understanding the gaps they create. This comprehension provides the foundation for negotiation strategies that can bridge these gaps, thereby fostering understanding, embracing diversity, and promoting unity. Understanding the world of others, after all, is the first step in making it a better place for everyone. As we journey further into this book, we shall delve into empathy's role in negotiation, as well as the tools and strategies available to negotiate effectively amidst these differences.

Chapter 4. Connective Dialogues: Empathy and Understanding in Negotiation

In the complex universe of negotiation, two elements emerge as a profound axis around which successful discussions revolve: empathy and understanding. With these keys, one can unlock doors to compromise, agreement, and harmony in the face of the potentials for discord.

4.1. The Importance of Empathy in Negotiation

Empathy, the art of recognizing, understanding, and sharing another's feelings, serves as a cornerstone in the architecture of negotiation. It accelerates the journey towards mutual agreements and paves the way for a more profound understanding of the other party's needs and desires.

Empathy's import comes from its ability to humanize discussions. It strips away the veneer of detachment that can permeate negotiations, allowing participants to engage with one another on a more personal, emotional level. This emotional proximity fosters an environment conducive to sharing, listening, and, ultimately, agreement.

When negotiators approach discussions with empathy, they communicate to the other party their willingness to understand their perspective, thereby building trust. This rapport makes it more likely that both sides will collaborate to create mutually beneficial outcomes.

4.2. Applying Empathy: A Step-by-Step Approach

There isn't a switch one can flick on to become empathetic instantly; empathy requires cultivation. Let's unpack a step-by-step approach to applying empathy during negotiations:

1. **Active Listening:** In any negotiation, listening is just as important, if not more so, than speaking. Active listening goes beyond merely hearing words — it involves interpreting and understanding the underlying sentiments.

2. **Validation:** After comprehending the other party's standpoint, it's crucial to validate their beliefs, concerns, and feelings. Validation doesn't necessarily mean agreeing but expressing that their perspective is valued and integral to the negotiation process.

3. **Reflection:** Reflect what you heard. This means echoing back the speaker's thoughts to demonstrate comprehension and allow clarification, if necessary.

4. **Questioning:** Ask open-ended questions. These types of questions amplify understanding and encourage further elucidation of viewpoints.

5. **Expressing Understanding:** After thoroughly hearing out the party, express your understanding of their stance. This assures them that their perspectives have been fully comprehended and incorporated into the negotiation process.

4.3. Understanding in Negotiation: The Cornerstone to Collaboration

Understanding weaves its magic within the tapestry of negotiation, creating a mutually collaborative atmosphere. When parties comprehend each other's point of view, it fast-tracks the identification of commonalities and, consequently, the possible intersection of interests. Understanding promotes reciprocity, motivating parties to respond in kind to actions that reflect mutual recognition.

Understanding, like empathy, can be fostered and applied systematically, let's delve into that:

4.4. Cultivating Understanding: A Systematic Approach

Understanding is not conjured from thin air, but rather nurtured through a systematic approach:

1. **Research:** Before negotiations commence, invest time in understanding the other party. This includes their goals, needs, constraints, societal, cultural, and personal context.

2. **Active Listening:** Understanding greatly benefits from empathetic listening—analyzing not only what is said but also the underlying meaning or intent.

3. **Non-Verbal Communication:** Pay attention to non-verbal cues and body language. These can provide insights into feelings, attitudes, and reactions.

4. **Open-ended Questions:** Use open-ended questions to encourage detailed answers, which add depth to understanding.

5. **Paraphrasing:** Restating what was said helps to clarify any misunderstanding and displays a willingness to understand.

Ultimately, understanding cannot be reached without empathy, and true empathy cannot be achieved without understanding. These two elements are intertwined, each feeding off and enriching the other.

4.5. Synergy Between Empathy and Understanding

The symbiotic relationship between empathy and understanding is undeniable. One cannot sincerely exist without the other during a negotiation. This relationship creates a space where each party feels heard, valued, and understood, thereby leaning into the heart of unifying negotiations.

Empathy without understanding may lead to compassionate gestures that miss the point of the other party's needs or concerns. Understanding without empathy risks being experienced as cold or uncaring. Together, they create an atmosphere that fosters open dialogue and effective negotiation.

This synergy results in constructive outcomes for both parties, radiating positive impacts throughout potential future interactions.

4.6. Conclusion

The labyrinth of negotiation can be navigated effectively when contestants harbor empathy and understanding. It encourages engagement on human terms rather than purely transactional ones, opening pathways to resolution that are both gratifying and enduring. Not only do these vital components enable successful negotiation, but they also sow the seeds for sustainable relationships.

By mastering the twin arts of empathy and understanding, we can cultivate a negotiation environment that transcends traditional bargaining, facilitating a co-creative process that bridges gaps and builds lasting connections. Each negotiation becomes not a battleground, but a garden ripe with potential for collaboration, compromise, and mutual growth—one that illuminates our shared humanity and spurs us onward to collective advancement.

Chapter 5. Tools of the Trade: Practical Strategies for Effective Negotiation

Delving into the world of negotiation, one cannot overlook the significance of having the right tools at one's disposal. Just as an artisan requires an array of tools to give shape to their vision on the canvas, similarly, an adept negotiator deploys a collection of strategies to pave the pathway towards mutual understanding and agreement.

5.1. The Power of Preparation

The stepping stone to effective negotiation is meticulous preparation. Rooted in understanding the crux of the dispute, participants' interests and the potential options for agreement, preparation encompasses thorough homework and planning. In this context, remember that the preparation phase involves more than merely reciting your viewpoints. Instead, it calls for constructive introspection, anticipating possible objections and counter-arguments, evaluating the underlying factors powering your opposition's stance, and setting a clear desired outcome.

An essential part of preparation is to know your BATNA (Best Alternative To a Negotiated Agreement). This concept, introduced by Roger Fisher and William Ury in their seminal work, "Getting to Yes", serves as your fallback plan and helps you to stay grounded during negotiation. Understanding your BATNA ensures that you have a plan B, preventing you from accepting unfavorable terms or pushing harder than necessary.

5.2. The Art of Listening

Active listening forms a cornerstone of successful negotiation. Its impact expands beyond merely comprehending the words of your negotiation partner. It involves a deep understanding of the person's feelings, needs, and desires transmitted through their verbal and non-verbal communication.

In order to make your negotiation partner feel heard and acknowledged, display empathetic body language and paraphrase their perspective to affirm your understanding. It fosters a positive exchange environment, making the counterpart more receptive to your viewpoint.

5.3. Leveraging Questioning Techniques

Ask targeted, open-ended questions that prompt your negotiation partner to divulge more about their position and interests. Such questions not only yield valuable information but also help in uncovering the underlying needs, concerns or fears, enabling you to suggest mutually satisfying solutions.

Here are some effective questioning strategies:

- Probing: To unwrap the layers of your negotiation partner's position or delve into a particular topic, use probing questions like, "Can you explain more about that point?"

- Clarifying: Carefully crafted clarifying questions can prevent misunderstandings. For instance, "Let's go back to your proposal about the distribution strategy. When you mention 'equitable division,' what exactly do you mean?"

- Hypothetical: These can be used as a guage to understand the other party's flexibility. For instance, "If we could arrange for a more flexible delivery schedule, would that make our proposal more appealing to you?"

5.4. Navigating Emotions

Emotions can often outweigh logic in a negotiation. An effective negotiator understands the influence of emotions, both their own and their partners. This requires being mindful of emotional reactions, managing these emotions, while also empathizing with the reactions of the other side. Maintaining a composed demeanor, empathizing when the other party is under emotional stress, and proposing a break when tension escalates, can go a long way in sustaining a constructive negotiation environment.

5.5. Framing the Negotiation

Objective framing of the negotiation situation plays a significant role in influencing the other party's perception and openness towards consensus. Highlighting shared interests, emphasizing potential mutual gains, or illustrating the consequences of non-agreement can steer negotiations towards resolution.

5.6. The Power of Concessions

To project a cooperative approach, one can strategically employ a concession strategy. While offering small, early concessions can set a cooperative tone, it is advisable to save significant concessions for later stages. Conveying the value of your concessions, and explaining how they meet your partner's interests, ensures you maximize their impact.

In conclusion, a skilled negotiator uses these practical tools not as weapons to overpower but as instruments of harmony. Each strategy should be deployed meticulously, sculpting the negotiation landscape towards a scenario of mutual consent and benefits, ultimately culminating into a unified resolution. The power of effective negotiation lies in its ability to transform seemingly insurmountable differences into harmonious agreements, hence fostering bridges of cooperation and understanding.

Chapter 6. Negotiation Across Cultures: Intersectionality and Its Impact

The chapter opens with a vital understanding that we live in a world steeped in diversity, curtained with myriad cultures, bounded by various ethnicities and stitched together with numerous distinct identities. Savvy negotiators know that negotiation is not a one-size-fits-all technique, but a dynamic process shaped by the complexities of human identities and societies. To navigate this labyrinth, we must first understand the concept of intersectionality and its relevance specifically to negotiation.

6.1. Intersectionality: A Necessary Prism

The proposition of intersectionality, conceived by Kimberlé Crenshaw in the 1980s, presents a transformative and radical way of viewing the world. It establishes that our identities are not separate threads but, instead, an intertwined and interconnected tapestry. Ethnicity, gender, class, religion, age, and other markers of identity intersect, creating a unique matrix of inequality or oppression depending on the context. This intricate dance of identities, the distinctions and commonalities, the disparities and similarities, all shape our experiences, our perspectives, and importantly for us, our negotiation approaches.

6.2. Navigating Cultural Landscapes in Negotiations

At the heart of every negotiation process is communication. Effective communication hinges on our cultural competence: the ability to recognize, understand, and respect the cultural differences that exist within our world. These differences often dictate the rules of engagement, the norms of communication, the values that underpin the negotiation objective, and the bargaining tactics employed.

In some cultures, directness and candity are favored, while other cultures might seek to work through subtler cues and non-verbal communication. Some societies value a competitive, zero-sum game approach, while others lean towards a cooperative, problem-solving tactic where harmony and group interest reign. As negotiators, it is our role to decode these cultural cues, understand their implications, and adapt our strategy accordingly.

Perception of time poses another significant cultural divergence. The Western world typically views time as a linear, finite entity, which influences a fast-paced, results-oriented negotiation style. Conversely, several Eastern societies regard time as a cyclical, infinite resource, thereby favoring a slower-paced, relationship-oriented negotiation approach.

Likewise, frameworks of hierarchy and power also hold significant sway over negotiation practices. While some cultures prefer a hierarchical structure where the superior decides, others opt for an egalitarian system that values consensus and equal participation.

6.3. Embracing Intersectionality in the Negotiation Room

Intersectionality provides us with a valuable tool to deconstruct our preconceived notions and biases about the 'other.' It allows us to enter the negotiation room with an open mind, eager to learn, adapt, and find common ground even amidst towering differences. We should strive to shift our perspective from viewing these cultural and intersectional differences as barriers to be overcome, to catalysts for developing innovative solutions, enriching our worldview, and fostering unity.

6.4. Intersectionality and Power: Balance in Negotiation

Power dynamics always pervade the negotiation table, and these dynamics often intersect along the lines of culture, ethnicity, gender, and other identity markers. Owing to cultural differences or biases, one identity might be consciously or unconsciously favored, resulting in an unequal negotiation environment. Interrogating these power structures, acknowledging these disparities, and seeking to correct them should be taken up actively by those at the negotiation table.

6.5. Implementing Intersectionality: Real-Life Scenarios and Case Studies

This final section presents a reflection on diverse real-life negotiations across cultures, exploring how an understanding and application of intersectionality not only led to successful outcomes but also forged stronger relationships and common understanding. Through a thorough examination of various case studies pertaining to international diplomacy, corporate negotiations, and interpersonal conflict resolution, readers are given a deep dive into the myriad ways intersectionality influences the negotiation process and its outcomes.

Looking through the lens of intersectionality gives us the insight to express empathy and understanding in negotiations across cultural divides. It is both our tool and our gift, allowing us to approach negotiation with a respect and recognition of the diverse threads of experience that we all carry and which shape our life stories. Only by embracing this approach can we seek to bridge the gap and build lasting, mutually beneficial agreements in our interconnected and beautifully complex world.

Chapter 7. Gender and Negotiation: Reducing the Gap with Effective Communication

The world of negotiation doesn't exist in isolation from societal structures. Gender, an integral part of these structures, significantly influences both direct and indirect communication styles across different negotiation scenarios. This chapter aims to investigate the nexus between gender and negotiation and provide effective strategies to navigate gendered nuances, ultimately enabling individuals to bridge communication gaps effectively.

7.1. Gendered Negotiation Styles

Gender, a notable influencing factor in the act of negotiation, often dictates its dynamics. Stereotypically, negotiation styles are bifurcated with men embracing a competitive, unyielding style and women adopting a cooperative, collaborative approach. However, it's crucial to understand that negotiators are not bound to these arbitrary lines. Negotiators can, and do, succeed employing styles that transcend traditional gender norms. After all, a negotiation is an act of persuading the other party to accept a mutually beneficial agreement; hence, flexibility is key.

But why do certain gendered tendencies emerge? Many societies condition individuals from a young age to conform to certain behavioral norms. Men are often encouraged to be assertive and commanding, thereby facilitating a dominant, competitive negotiation style. Conversely, women are conventionally taught to be nurturing and communal, leading to a collaborative, cooperative negotiation style. Such innate societal patterns shape underlying negotiation practices across genders and thus must be recognized and addressed to foster more equitable discussions.

7.2. Interplay of Gender Bias in Negotiations

Bias, often unconscious, infiltrates every stratum of our lives, including negotiations. Within the negotiation sphere, these biases can manifest subtly and dramatically alter the negotiation's outcome. One prevalent impact of gender bias is the unequal judgment of assertiveness in negotiation. Women who exhibit assertiveness, a celebrated trait in negotiators, may experience backlash as this trait challenges traditional gender norms. Men, on the other hand, wielding assertiveness are often commended.

Negotiators must regularly introspect and challenge these inherent biases to ensure fairness in negotiations. Illuminating and addressing these biases fosters a more inclusive negotiation space that values diverse voices and negotiation styles equally.

7.3. Tools for Bridging the Gap

Building awareness around gendered negotiation dynamics is the first step towards fostering more equitable negotiations; the next is arming ourselves with practical tools to bridge this gap.

1. **Language**: Communication is key in negotiation. The language utilized can significantly sway the course and outcome of the negotiation. Neutral, inclusive language helps establish respect, understanding, and breaks down any gender-based barriers.

2. **Assertiveness training**: Recognition and practice of assertiveness skills, sans the gender bias, can transform the negotiation landscape. It encourages negotiators to embrace a balanced, measured assertiveness, regardless of gender.

3. **Bias education**: Heightened awareness and education about bias can help individuals identify bias, consciously and unconsciously, in negotiations and act to rectify them.

7.4. Overcoming Gender Barriers in Negotiations: Case Studies

Equipping ourselves with theoretical knowledge and tools is a great starting point. Still, viewing these concepts in action through real-life examples further substantiates the importance of gender-conscious negotiation strategies.

1. **Case Study 1**: A negotiation between a company's senior female executive and male stakeholders provides insights into how the executive effectively navigated the negotiation, despite gender stereotypes.

2. **Case Study 2**: A sales negotiation involving a male salesperson and female client demonstrates the importance of bias awareness and equal assertiveness during negotiations.

7.5. Gender, Communication, and Future Negotiations

While substantial progress has been made, more work is needed to bridge the gender gap in negotiations effectively. The future of negotiation is intrinsically linked with evolving gender norms. As societies mature and gender roles further dissolve, the negotiation space will inevitably reflect this progress. It calls for an increased focus on gender-equitable negotiation education and practices.

In conclusion, the intersection of gender and negotiations offers an arena ripe for exploration and growth. Recognizing gendered negotiation tendencies, challenging biases, and arming oneself with suitable tools significantly enhances negotiation's efficacy and outcomes. It encourages the bridging of differences and fosters unity, understanding, and progress. Despite societal conditioning and deeply ingrained stereotypes, each negotiation attempt provides us an opportunity to enact change, thereby reducing the gap in gender and negotiation, one conversation at a time. After all, negotiation is an art, a powerful tool for effecting change and bridging disparities. It's time we wield this tool without the baggage of gender biases, paving the way towards an equitable future.

Chapter 8. Power Dynamics: Handling and Balancing Influences in Negotiation

Power is an inherently complex and multifaceted concept that plays a significant role in every negotiation process. It can be concealed and subtle, or it can be overt and imposing. Having the ability to perceive, utilize, and balance power in a negotiation can be the difference between a deadlock and a successful resolution. It is precisely the understanding and strategic deployment of power that forms the backbone of this chapter. Hence, let's delve into the labyrinth of power dynamics in negotiation.

8.1. Grasping Power: Sources and Types

If we want to successfully maneuver through the power dynamics at play in negotiation, we must first understand what power is. Power, as it pertains to negotiation, can be seen as a party's capacity to influence the actions, decisions, or thinking of another party. A diverse array of factors can confer this capacity, leading to various types of power.

Some negotiators derive power from their position or authority within a company or institution. This is known as positional power, and it is perhaps the most readily apparent form of power. However, power isn't always defined by job titles or hierarchical standing.

Expert power stems from one's specialized knowledge or expertise, while referent power comes from the respect and admiration one commands from others. Reward power emanates from the ability to dispense rewards, while coercive power is drawn from the potential to impose penalties or withhold benefits. Personal power, on the other hand, is not connected to any external factor but lies solely within the individual. It comes from one's skills, capabilities, and, ultimately, confidence.

8.2. Asserting Power: Tactics and Techniques

Once we understand the types of power at play, we can explore how to leverage them effectively. The mere possession of power is not enough; how you wield it determines your success in negotiation.

Firstly, it's crucial to maintain a level of flexibility. Power is not static, and holding onto power in negotiations requires adaptability. This might mean changing your strategy, reevaluating your position, or shifting your desired outcomes as the negotiation evolves.

One effective technique is to use your sources of power to frame the negotiation and guide its trajectory. For instance, if you hold expert power, position yourself as the authority, provide insightful information, and influence the conversation based on your expertise.

Positional power can be exerted through setting the agenda, determining the negotiation's pace, and stipulating its boundaries. However, it's essential to wield this power with a balance of assertiveness and diplomacy. Overly aggressive tactics can cause the other party to become defensive and impede the negotiation.

Nonetheless, it's crucial to remember that exerting power doesn't always mean dominating the conversation. In fact, one of the most potent forms of power is the power to listen and understand the other party's perspective genuinely.

8.3. Balancing Power: Creating Equitable Negotiation Environments

Power imbalance is a common challenge in negotiations. While it's virtually impossible to ensure both sides have equal power, striving for a balance can foster productive and respectful conversations.

If you find yourself with less power, look for ways to increase your leverage. You could enhance your negotiation power by building alliances, increasing your knowledge on the subject in question, or presenting alternative solutions that may appeal to the other party.

In situations where you hold more power, exercising empathy and respect is paramount. Not only does this help maintain a constructive atmosphere, but it also increases the likelihood of the other party accepting the outcome, leading to longer-lasting resolutions.

Mutually beneficial negotiations are not about 'win and lose.' They are about creating value for all parties involved. In essence, power should not be about domination; it should be about fostering collaboration and mutual understanding.

8.4. In Search of Equality: Power Dynamics and Ethics

With power dynamics comes the pressing concern of ethics. A negotiator should always strive to conduct negotiations ethically, ensuring transparency, honesty, and fairness.

Overusing power can lead to unethical behaviors such as manipulation, coercion, or intimidation. These actions hold severe consequences, including deteriorating relationships and fostering mistrust. They also discourage open communication, undermining the negotiation process itself.

Negotiations that uphold the highest ethical standards not only yield desirable results but also forge resilient relationships and create an environment conducive to resolution in future conflicts.

In essence, handling and balancing power dynamics in negotiation require an intricate blend of understanding, strategy, adaptability, and ethics. Extracting the potency inherent in these dynamics can transform negotiations into tools for bridging gaps, forging connections, and fostering progress.

Chapter 9. From Impasse to Progress: Overcoming Roadblocks in Negotiation

Negotiation is fascinating, filled with an array of innate complexities; it's almost like unfolding origami, where each crease provides a novel perspective, hidden in plain sight. Often, in the labyrinth of offers, discussions, and perceived gains, we encounter deadlocks, a situation fondly referred to as an 'impasse.' To help you navigate these impasses and guide you on the path of progress, we've devised this intricate exploration.

9.1. The Anatomy of an Impasse

Negotiations, like rivers, can be unpredictable and volatile. Negotiators, acting as skillful navigators, must confront these precarious situations and establish harmony. An impasse, much akin to a river's rock, obstructs the smooth flow of conversation, creating ripples. In essence, an impasse in negotiation occurs when all parties reach a stalemate, unable to proceed further due to conflicting interests, lack of common ground, or innumerable other obstructions.

Impasses can reside in three primary arenas: tangibles, communication, and emotions. Tangibles pertain to the actual subject matter of the negotiation; divergence here can stem from insuperable differences concerning the negotiation details. Communication-based impasses arise from misunderstandings or lack of transparency. Lastly, emotional impasses stem from biases, ego battles, or negative history between the negotiating parties.

9.2. Decoding the Impasse: Diagnosing the Roadblocks

Before finding solutions, it is pivotal to pinpoint the problem. Is the impasse due to divergent interests? Or, is it a manifestation of a deeper discord? Evoking our understanding of the anatomy of an impasse, we can deploy a three-dimension diagnostic tool:

1. Unearth the Tangibles: Explore the tangible aspects of the negotiation and inspect where the divergence emerged. Is there scope for trade-offs or altering interests?

2. Decode the Communication: Analyze the dialogue carefully. Are there any misunderstandings that need clarification? Are there hidden issues that are left unaddressed?

3. Douse the Emotions: Acknowledge the emotional undertones. Are there biases or negative emotions shaping the conversation? What can be done to pacify these?

9.3. Plotting the Navigational Route: Strategies to Overcome Impasses

With an understanding of the nature of impasse and a diagnostic mechanism in place, it's time to equip ourselves with strategies to overcome these obstacles and continue our journey towards successful negotiation.

1. Seek the BATNA: Best Alternative to a Negotiated Agreement (BATNA) is a powerful concept. It provides a feasible alternative when negotiation reaches a stalemate.

2. Involve a Mediator: Neutral, third-party intervention often helps to recalibrate the negotiation, offer fresh perspective, or control escalated emotions.

3. Initiate Interest-Based Negotiation: Emphasize shared interests over conflicting positions. This refocusing can pave the way to find common ground.

4. Subdivide the Problem: Divide the larger problem into smaller, more manageable chunks. Doing so may prevent overwhelming or intimidating scenarios.

5. Utilize Time as a Tool: Sometimes, simply taking a break can diffuse tensions, provide time for reassessment, and lead to smoother conversations.

9.4. At the Helm: Practical Case Studies

The true caliber of a strategy comes forth when it is employed on the ground, in the heat of the battle called negotiation. Let us observe a couple of real-life case studies where these strategies turned an impending doom into a viable path forward.

Case Study 1: The International Trade War

The recent international trade war was a formidable negotiation impasse. Using the BATNA strategy, nations explored alternatives to the deadlock and found ways to continue international trade, often through re-negotiation or finding new trade partners. It showcased how BATNA could provide alternatives and keep channels open, even in the face of colossal deadlocks.

Case Study 2: The Corporate Merger

The merger between two corporate giants had hit a roadblock due to a vast difference in valuation perception. A professional mediator stepped in and helped facilitate multi-tier discussions involving board members, stakeholders, and employees. This monumental task was overcome through systematic negotiations, demonstrating the power of a neutral mediator in handling complex negotiations.

9.5. Beyond the Impasse: The Journey Ahead

Navigating through a negotiation impasse is an arduous journey. However, with a robust understanding of the underlying issues, keen diagnostic prowess, and an arsenal of time-tested strategies, this journey can lead to mutually beneficial results, even in the face of seemingly insurmountable roadblocks. Demonstrated time and again, through trials by fire in the crucible of real-life negotiations, these strategies have emerged victorious; a testimony to their potential in bridging divides and securing progress. As we journey forward, may the beacon of effective negotiation always illuminate our paths, guiding us towards resolution, consensus, and harmony.

Chapter 10. Building Bridges: Case Studies of Successful Negotiations

The bridge of negotiation is both a marvelous artistry and a dynamic discipline, molded by the simultaneous dance of humanity's flair for communication and ability to understand. Building this symbolic bridge, piece by piece, can transform heated debates into harmonious arrangements, and divergent viewpoints into united visions. In this chapter, we delve into the practical exemplification of these abstract concepts through illustrations of real-world success in various contexts of negotiation. We traverse across various domains - from corporate boardrooms to international diplomacy, ensuring a rich panorama that elucidates the universality of negotiation.

10.1. A Black and White Agreement in Full Color: The Success of the NFL Players Strike in 2011

The year was 2011, and the professional football landscape in America was fraught with tension. The players, organized under the National Football League Players Association (NFLPA), were on strike. It was the consequence of a labor dispute that emanated from disagreements on varied points - ranging from player safety, revenue sharing, to the structure of contracts, among others. This standoff threatened the very existence of the upcoming NFL season.

But what transpired was an example of brilliant negotiation that turned this disagreement into an agreement that still stands today. The players and the league owners had to put their differences aside, and embark on an arduous journey of identifying common grounds, recognizing interdependences, finding creative solutions and above all, exhibiting a sense of mutual respect and understanding. Building the bridge of discussion over raging rivers of discord, both parties successfully negotiated through the obstacles, resulting in a 10-year collective bargaining agreement. It was a model example illustrating that the art of negotiation isn't about winning or losing, but about finding the middle ground for sustained mutual benefits.

10.2. Uniting Nations for Climate Action: The Paris Agreement

Environs of Le Bourget in Paris, France, bore witness to a different kind of battle in December, 2015. Representatives from 196 nations congregated under the single roof of the Paris Climate Conference to negotiate on humankind's response against the devastating impacts of climate change. Their aim was to jointly commit to limit global warming to well below 2 degrees Celsius above pre-industrial levels.

This challenge wasn't merely about the technical details of carbon emission cuts or financial contributions. It was a negotiation confluence where different political ideologies, economic strati, and comprehension of climate science had to be woven into a robust, yet flexible agreement. Through persistent negotiation, nations overcame their differences and built a common understanding. The result: The Paris Agreement, an unprecedented global effort for climate action.

The agreement was built on the foundation of communication and negotiation, demonstrating that when the stakes are global, negotiation acts as the cement to unify diversified national interests towards a common cause.

10.3. The High Stakes Gamble: IBM's Negotiations for Survival

In the realm of business, the art of negotiation is often pivotal for survival and success. Let's rewind to the early 1990s when IBM, a renowned American multinational technology company, found itself in dire financial straits. What saved the day was an astute act of negotiation between IBM and its employees.

Facing the possibility of a major downsizing, IBM introduced the 'Employee Buyout Plan'. This innovative solution gave employees an option to voluntarily leave the company with an attractive severance package, ensuring a respectful exit, and alleviating the company's financial burdens simultaneously. The gamble paid off. Instead of forcing an unpopular decision, IBM negotiated a path that at once respected the needs of its employees and catered to its own survival.

This case study encapsulates the power of negotiation within a corporate framework, reinforcing the fact that building bridges is possible even when the firm ground of financial stability trembles underneath.

These case studies span different fields, each with their unique challenges, yet the constant thread that weaves them into successful outcomes is the power of negotiation. They exemplify the fact that no gap is too wide, no bridge too far when individuals, corporations, nations come to the table ready to negotiate. Embracing this power, we can hope to successfully navigate through any conflict, all the while building bridges of understanding, respect, and mutual gain.

Chapter 11. The Future of Negotiation: Trends, Technology, and Tomorrow

We stand now at the conflux of a rapidly changing world, where developments in technology, shifts in global power structures, and evolving societal norms are fundamentally transforming the landscape of negotiation. This chapter ventures to dissect these changes and project the future of negotiation tactics, tools, and trends.

11.1. The Technological Revolution in Negotiation

The digital age has broached new frontiers for negotiations, equipping negotiators with the tools and platforms to converse, connect, and resolve conflicts in innovative ways. Digital technology has shattered geographical barriers, enabling negotiators to interact with counterparts from different locations, countries, and even time zones through video conferencing and other virtual communication tools.

Artificial Intelligence (AI) is emerging as a powerful ally in negotiations, capable of providing negotiators with critical inputs such as data analysis, market trends, and predictive modeling. The AI-powered negotiation bots have already begun to augment the negotiation process by streamlining tasks, increasing efficiency, and improving decision-making processes. However, the rising use of AI calls for ethical considerations and the establishment of clear boundaries and standards to ensure fair and equal negotiation outcomes.

Blockchain technology also holds promise for negotiation by introducing a new level of transparency and security. Smart contracts powered by blockchain technology could potentially eliminate the need for intermediary parties, thus simplifying the negotiation process. Technology, while being a tool for empowerment, also presents challenges such as those related to privacy concerns, data security, and digital literacy which need to be addressed as we tread forward.

11.2. Global Trends Impacting Negotiation

In the global arena, the rise of emerging markets, the shift of economic power towards the east, and the escalating importance of climate change negotiations are shaping new paradigms for negotiation.

Emerging economies like China, India, and Brazil are gaining increased leverage in international negotiations due to their robust economies and fast-growing consumer markets. This shift is compelling negotiators from established economies to reassess their strategies and engage effectively with these newer players.

Climate change negotiations are another significant arena driving shifts in negotiation strategies. The urgency to address environmental concerns has steered the negotiation tables towards co-operative, value-creating solutions that emphasize shared benefits.

11.3. Shifts in Societal Norms and Its Implications

Evolving societal norms like inclusivity and the quest for gender balance have also irrefutably influenced the negotiation landscape.

The quest for gender balance in negotiation rooms is not just a moral requirement but also a practical necessity due to the historically proven advantage of diverse perspectives. Similarly, inclusivity in negotiations facilitates more comprehensive and more acceptable outcomes, ensuring that every voice is heard and valued.

11.4. Looking Towards Tomorrow: Future Skills for Negotiators

In view of the evolving landscape, negotiation skills must also adapt and innovate. Key competencies such as digital literacy, cultural intelligence, emotional intelligence, ethical discernment, and collaborative problem-solving emerge as essential future skills for effective negotiation.

Moreover, there is an increasing awareness of the importance of gender and cultural nuances in negotiations. Negotiators, therefore, need to understand these and be competent in adapting their negotiation strategies accordingly.

Emotional intelligence, a blend of self-awareness, self-management, social awareness, and relationship management, is also becoming increasingly important for modern negotiators. It enables us to strike a balance between result-oriented negotiations and empathetic human connections, a balance that fosters meaningful, lasting agreements.

As we brush the surface of the future of negotiation, we realize the magnitude and complexity of the upcoming changes. Yet, amidst the flux, the fundamental essence of negotiation remains - the pursuit of understanding, empathy, and collaborative problem solving. Empowered by technological progress, molded by threads of global influence, and shaped by the evolving norms of society, we march towards a future where negotiation continues to be a powerful tool for bridging differences, fostering unity, and catalyzing progress.

www.ingramcontent.com/pod-product-compliance
Lightning Source LLC
Chambersburg PA
CBHW070139230526
45472CB00004B/1607